All Good & Holy People

Prayers for Grieving and Remembering Loved Ones

TWENTY-THIRD PUBLICATIONS
twentythirdpublications.com

Design and layout: Jessica Llewellyn

Published in Canada by Novalis
as ***Praying November***

Publishing Office
1 Eglinton Ave East, Suite 800
Toronto, Ontario, Canada
M4P 3A1

Head Office
4475 Frontenac Street
Montréal, Québec, Canada
H2H 2S2

www.novalis.ca

ISBN (for Canada):
978-2-89688-822-1

Published in the United States
by Twenty-Third Publications,
A Division of Bayard, Inc. as
All Good and Holy People

One Montauk Avenue, Suite 200
New London, CT 06320
Tel: (860) 437-3012 or (800) 321-0411

www.twentythirdpublications.com

ISBN (for USA):
978-1-62785-543-3

Cover design: Jeff McCall
Cover photo: ©Smileus /
Shutterstock.com

Prayer references can be found at the back of the book.

Cataloguing in Publication is available from Library and Archives Canada.

Photos: Shutterstock: p. 12, 16, 22, 30, 50; iStock: p. 6, 8, 36, 40, 46

We acknowledge the support of the Government of Canada.

Printed in Canada.

5 4 3 2 1   24 23 22 21 20

MIX
Paper from responsible sources
FSC® C103567

Table of Contents

In Memoriam

Name	Date

He restores
my soul.
Psalm 23.3

Introduction

The month of November is traditionally when the Church remembers those that have died. During this month, we are invited to pray for our family members and friends who have passed away, whether they died recently or a longer time ago.

The month begins with All Saints' Day (Nov 1), during which we commemorate women and men who committed themselves to a great degree of holiness in their personal lives and witnessed to the saving power of Christ's death and resurrection in a special way.

On Nov 2, we commemorate All Souls' Day, that is, we pray for all of the faithful departed. On this day in particular, all Catholics pray for the dead.

The booklet you hold in your hands is an aid to help you celebrate this month. Page 4 gives you space to write down the special people in your life that you wish to remember and pray for this month. The pages throughout include a wide range of prayers for various occasions, which you can pray to commemorate your lost loved ones. Whether your loss is more immediate and you are struggling with feelings of grief, loss and hopelessness, or you are simply commemorating special anniversaries of loved ones who died a while ago, in this booklet you will find the prayers you need for this special month of prayer.

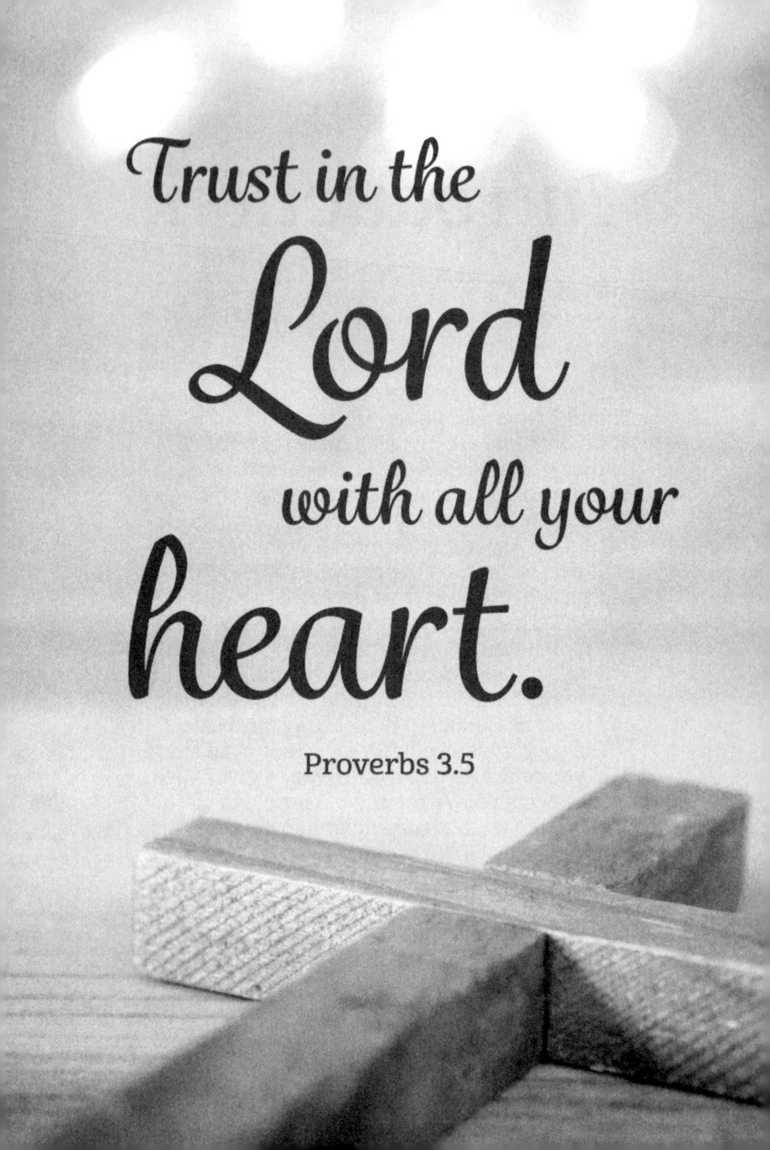
Trust in the
Lord
with all your
heart.
Proverbs 3.5

Prayer for Those Who Are Dying

Prayer for Those Who Are Dying

O Holy Spirit,
the soul's most welcome guest,
pour out your love
on all those who are dying.
Comfort and sustain them
in their suffering and fear;
fill them with your peace
in their final moments.
Let your joy fill them as they draw closer
to the heavenly banquet.
And with mercy, accompany them
as they run to greet our Savior, Jesus Christ.
Amen.

Prayers for Those Who Have Died

Prayer for the Recently Deceased

Loving God,
during this time of great sorrow
come to comfort me.
During this time of my loss
take my loved one to be with you.
Embrace my loved one in your tender care,
and bring them to a place of eternal rest.
As for us, who are left behind in sadness,
wipe our tears of sorrow;
fill us with hope
and peace everlasting.
In Jesus' name I pray.
Amen.

Prayers for Those Who Have Died

God our Father,
your power brings us to birth,
your providence guides our lives,
and by your command we return to dust.
Lord, those who die still live in your presence;
their lives change but do not end.
I pray in hope for my family, relatives and friends,
and for all the dead known to you alone.
In company with Christ,
who died and now lives,
may they rejoice in your kingdom,
where all our tears are wiped away.
Unite us together again in one family,
to sing your praise forever and ever.
Amen.

God of love and kindness,
by the mystery of the cross
your Son, Jesus, conquered sin and death.
Look kindly upon your servant ______________.
Cleanse him/her of sin,
and grant him/her the joy of eternal life.
Amen.

Blessed
is the one who
trusts
in the Lord,
whose confidence
is in him.

Jeremiah 17.7

Prayers from the Saints

Prayer for the Dead

Receive in tranquility and peace, O Lord,
the souls of your servants
who have departed this present life to come to you.
Grant them rest
and place them in the habitations of light,
the abodes of blessed spirits.
Give them the life that will not age,
good things that will not pass away,
delights that have no end,
through Jesus Christ our Lord.
Amen.

Saint Ignatius of Antioch

A Wonderful Birth

Death is the ultimate grace
and the culmination of our Christian life.
It is not the end, as too many think,
but the beginning of a wonderful birth.
It marks not the end of a creature,
but their true development,
their full realization in love.
It fulfills our belonging in God's life,
removing the barriers that, here on Earth,
prevent us from enjoying life in God completely.
Death slows us to attend freely
to Love Eternal,
to be aware that Love gives itself to us
and to live in God forever...
When I think about my approaching death,
I say to myself,
"Good – soon I will see God!"

Venerable Marthe Robin

Prayer

Grant me, O Lord my God,
a mind to know you,
a heart to seek you,
wisdom to find you,
conduct pleasing to you,
faithful perseverance in waiting for you
and a hope of finally embracing you.
Amen.

Saint Thomas Aquinas

Lord, Bless All People

Lord, bless all who are filled with sadness.
Bless the broken spirits of those who suffer,
the oppressive solitude of the lonely people,
the person who knows no rest,
the suffering that we confide to no one.

Bless the procession
of night owls
that do not fear the specter
of unknown roads.
Bless the sufferings of those
who are dying this day.
Dear God, give them
a good death.

Bless hearts, Lord,
hearts that are bitter.
Above all,
comfort the sick,
teach forgetfulness to those
who have lost the one they love most.
Leave no one on the whole earth
in distress.

Bless those who are full of joy,
and protect them, Lord.
So far, you have never
delivered me from sadness.
It sometimes weighs heavily on me,
but you give me your strength
and so I can bear it.
Amen.

Saint Teresa Benedicta of the Cross

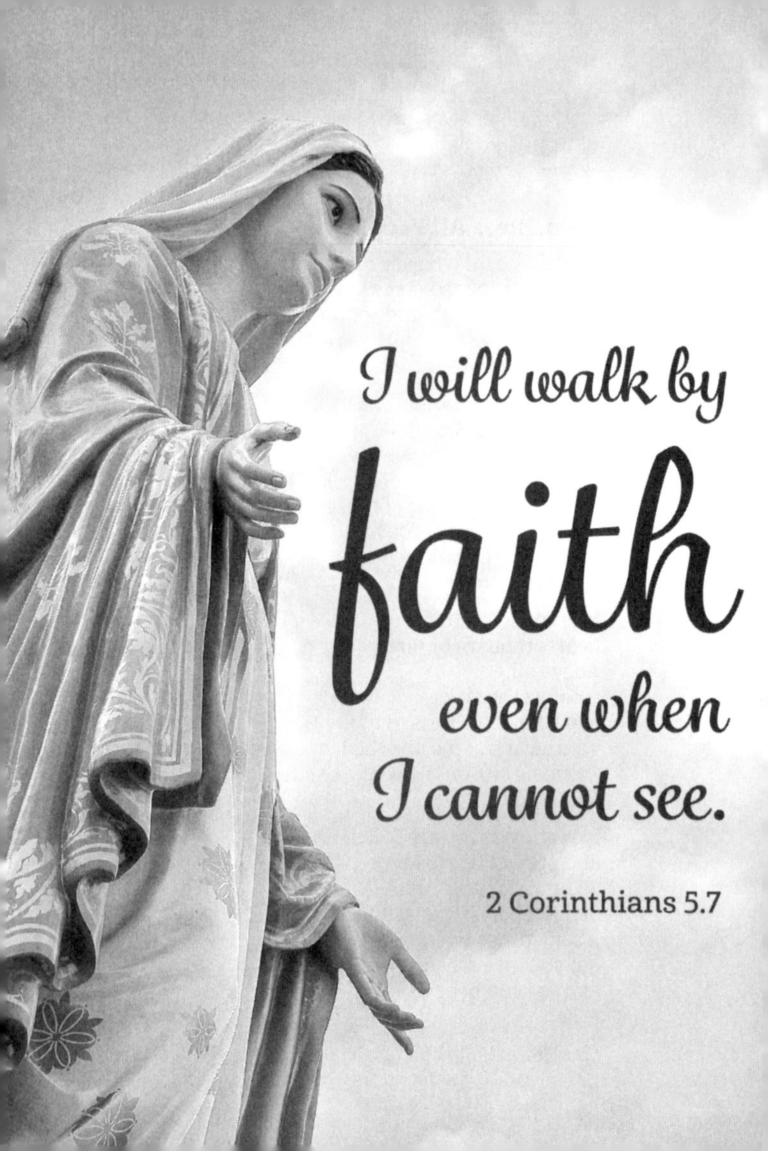
I will walk by
faith
even when
I cannot see.
2 Corinthians 5.7

Prayers to Mary

Prayer to the Immaculate Heart of Mary

O Most Blessed Mother,
heart of love, heart of mercy,
ever listening, caring, consoling,
hear our prayer.

As your children,
we implore your intercession
with Jesus your Son.
Receive with understanding and compassion
the petitions we place before you today,
especially... *(special intention).*

We are comforted in knowing
your heart is ever open
to those who ask for your prayer.
We entrust to your gentle care and intercession
those whom we love
and who are sick or lonely or hurting.

Help all of us, Holy Mother,
to bear our burdens in this life
until we may share eternal life and peace
with God forever.
Amen.

Prayer to Mary, Help of Christians

Most holy and Immaculate Virgin,
Help of Christians,
we place ourselves
under your motherly protection.
Throughout the Church's history
you have helped Christians
in times of trial, temptation, and danger.
Time and time again,
you have proven to be the Refuge of sinners,
the Hope of the hopeless,
the Consoler of the afflicted,
and the Comforter of the dying.

We promise to be faithful disciples
of Jesus Christ, your Son,
to proclaim his Good News
of God's love for all people,
and to work for peace and justice in our world.
With faith in your intercession,
we pray for the Church,
for our family and friends,
for the poor and abandoned,
and all the dying.
Grant, O Mary, Help of Christians,
the graces of which we stand in need.
(Mention your intentions.)

May we serve Jesus
with fidelity and love until death.
Help us and our loved ones
to attain the boundless joy
of being forever with our Father in heaven.
Mary, Help of Christians, pray for us!
Amen.

Prayer to Mary, Untier of Knots

Holy Mary, with all simplicity and patience
you have given us an example
of how to untangle the knots
in our complicated lives.

By being our mother forever,
you arrange and make clear the path
that unites us to Our Lord.
Holy Mary, Mother of God and ours,
with your maternal heart
untie the knots that upset our lives.
We ask you to receive in your hands
and deliver us from the chains and confusions
that have us restrained.

Blessed Virgin Mary, through your grace,
your intercession, and by your example,
deliver us from evil and untie the knots
that keep us from uniting with God,
so that once free of every confusion and error,
we may find him in all things,
have him in our hearts,
and serve him always in our brothers and sisters.
Mother of Good Counsel, pray for us.
Amen.

Prayer to Our Lady of Guadalupe

Dear Mother, we love you.
We thank you for your promise
to help us in our need.
We trust in your love
that dries our tears and comforts us.
Teach us to find our peace
in your Son, Jesus,
and bless us every day of our lives.
Help us to build a shrine in our hearts.
Make it as beautiful
as the one built for you
on the Mount of Tepeyac.
A shrine full of trust, hope,
and love of Jesus
growing stronger each day.

Mary, you have chosen to remain with us
by giving us
your most wonderful and holy self-image
on Juan Diego's cloak.
May we feel your loving presence
as we look upon your face.
Like Juan, give us the courage
to bring your message of hope to everyone.
You are our mother and our inspiration.
Hear our prayers and answer us.
Amen.

Prayer in Times of Trouble

Holy Virgin Mary,
you are reigning in glory, with Jesus, your Son.
Remember us in our sadness.
Look kindly on all who are suffering
or fighting against any difficulty.
Have pity on those who are separated
from someone they love.
Have pity on the loneliness of our hearts.
Have pity on the weakness of our faith and love.
Have pity on those who are weeping,
on those who are praying,
on those who are fearful.
Holy Mother, please obtain for all of us
hope and peace with justice.
Amen.

The Memorare

Remember, O most gracious Virgin Mary,
that never was it known
that anyone who fled to your protection,
implored your help,
or sought your intercession,
was left unaided.
Inspired with this confidence, I fly to you,
O Virgin of virgins, my Mother;
to you do I come, before you I stand,
sinful and sorrowful.
O mother of the Word Incarnate,
despise not my petitions,
but in your mercy hear and answer me.
Amen.

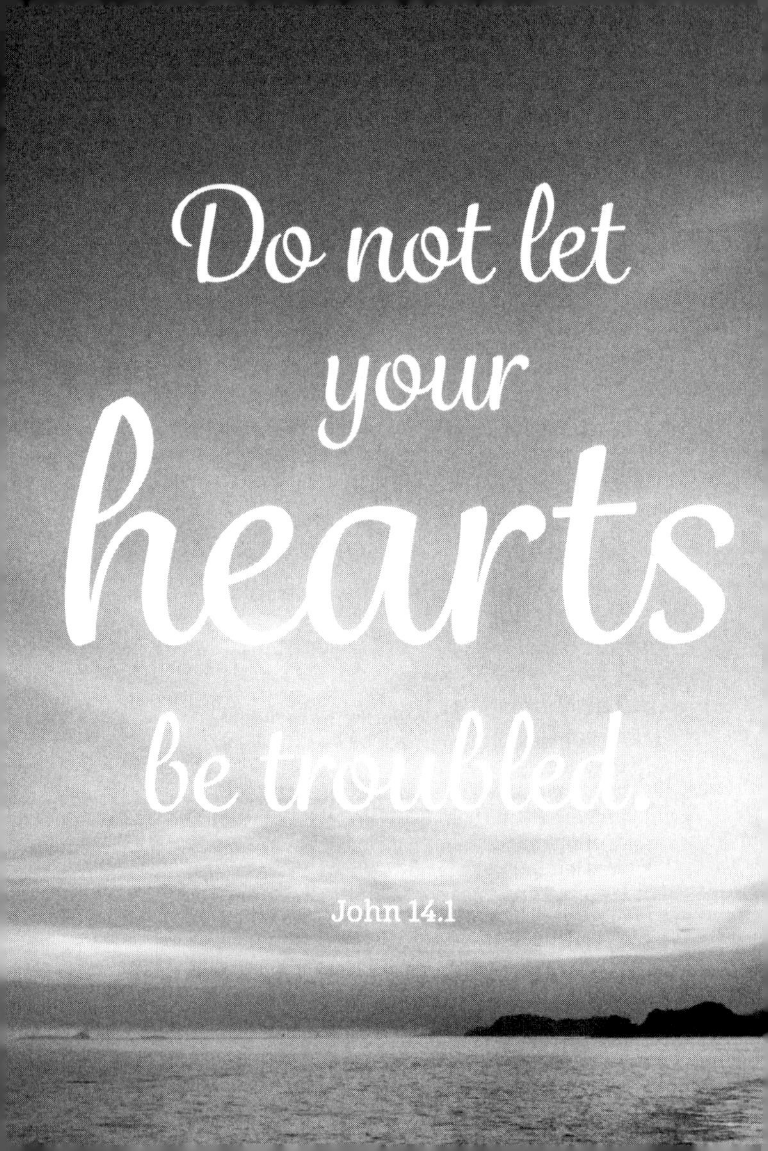
Do not let
your
hearts
be troubled.
John 14.1

When Grieving

On Grieving

Compassionate God,
I know that you share my grief,
see my tears,
and enter the hollowness
within me now.
I am ambushed by grief.
It stalks me and appears unexpectedly
along my path.
It is hard to imagine moving forward,
or beyond.

Be tender with me, God.
Let me know that I am not alone.
Give me words to repeat my story,
and give me patience with those
who ask me how I'm doing.
Open them to my honesty.
There is no one way to grieve.
Help me to believe that.
Amen.

Loss

O God of Consolation,
we come before you today bowed down by grief.
In mourning for what has been lost,
we carry our own pain
as well as that of others who have been affected.
We believe that when we suffer,
you enter into our suffering.
Even when we feel most alone,
we know that you never abandon us.

Strengthen our faith in your presence
at this time of loss.
Sanctify our tears;
heal our broken hearts.
When the time is right,
show us what needs to be done in order to
move forward.
Experiences of grief and loss
remind us of our utter dependence on you.

In the name of your Son, Jesus,
who suffered and died for us,
have mercy on us all.
Amen.

Prayer in a Time of Sadness or Grief

You are my friend and my protector, Lord.
You are almighty God.
The sun may not rise unless you will it,
nor the ocean cast its waves upon the shore.
As you know the shape of every living thing
 you have created,
you know each twist and turn of my heart.
You are beside me now in my suffering.
Your presence fills me with strength.
Be my source of light and life,
O Lord, forever - for always.
Amen.

Let Go and Let God

God of peace and acceptance,
things do not often go the way we want them to go.
We can be disappointed,
particularly when we want something really badly
and it doesn't work out.
We pray today to be granted the ability
to accept things that we are not able to change.
We pray for peace of mind and heart.
Please grant us the faith to trust in you.
Help us to follow the words in the Serenity Prayer:
"God, grant me the serenity
to accept the things I cannot change,
courage to change the things I can,
and wisdom to know the difference."
Amen.

Remembering Our Loved Ones

Dear God,
we thank you for the wonderful memories
we have of our departed loved ones.
We are grateful when these memories
bring us happiness and comfort.
Help us to continue to keep
the memories of our loved ones alive
by living out the gifts and virtues
we treasured so much in their lives.
May our remembrance of them
in this way help their spirit to live on in us,
and may the virtues contribute to building
your kingdom here on earth.
Amen.

Embracing Our Own Crosses

Dear Jesus,
When life presents us with difficulties and pain,
help us to look to your own suffering and be strengthened.
Your passion, death and resurrection
help us to embrace our own suffering.
When we confront obstacles that cause us to suffer,
we feel your presence and begin anew.
When we are the victims of injustice,
you carry our cross with us.
Jesus, continue to give us strength, comfort,
and consolation.
With you we can overcome all suffering.
Amen.

Prayer for Those Who Mourn

Gentle and compassionate God,
you hear the pleading cry
of those who mourn.
The death of _____________ reminds us
how precious the gift of life is
and calls to mind the saving power
of your Son, Jesus.
Please surround _____________'s family
and friends with love,
and give them the strength
needed to meet the challenges
of the days to come.
In Christ, may their sorrow be comforted
and their doubts fade.
May they be blessed now and always,
through Christ our Lord.
Amen.

Prayer for a Difficult Anniversary

God of consolation,
today marks an anniversary that dredges up
hurt, pain, grief and loss.
As another year comes to a close around this time,
mend my wounded heart.
Restore peace to our family
and renew our hope in you.
May memory not harden into fear and anger,
but soften into compassion and mercy.
With hope in your steadfast love, I pray.
Amen.

Lord, Help Us to Journey with Those Who Are Suffering

Healing God,
we witness suffering every day.
We pray today that you will extend
your healing touch to our loved ones.
Help us to recognize
that even in our darkest moments
you are always there for us,
as you were when your own Son suffered.
Grant us the wisdom and compassion
to serve as your instruments here on earth
as we walk beside those who are suffering.
May we be a source of light
in their darkest times
and a source of strength
in their weakest times.
We ask this through Jesus,
who made the greatest sacrifice in love
and service to us.
Amen.

Creed for a Hopeless Day

I believe
that the sun will rise again tomorrow.

I believe
that God loves his creation,
so thus I am loved
(even if I don't feel it).

I believe
that my past
will still be my past,
and that my future (whatever it is)
still awaits me.

I believe
that even though everything feels different
after today,
it cannot possibly be totally different.

So, God, in this day of shaken faith,
of rattled reality, of hopeless thinking,
remind me again that you are good,
that your creation is good,
and that life, even mine
on this day,
is good.
Amen.

I can do all things
through
Christ
who strengthens me.

Philippians 4.13

Family

Prayer at the Wake/Funeral of a Spouse

Strong God,
the stillness is broken only by my tears.
My cherished one has died.
Waves of words spill over me.
"My sympathy."
"Sorry for your loss."
"If there is anything we can do..."
The handshakes and the hugs
complete a circle of loss
that has my beloved as its center.
When we process to that space
where so often my beloved bowed in prayer,
our faith, too, has a word to say:
"Life is changed, not ended."
The waves of grief still engulf me,
but I cling to that promise.
I am exhausted.
Hold me tight, God.
I trust the tide of your grace
to return me to the safety of the shore.
Amen.

Prayer for a Death in the Family

Merciful God,
be with us as we mourn the death of ______________.
Such a loss is not easy to bear
and I pray for comfort and consolation.
May the promise of life with you
give us reason to hope,
and provide a pathway
through our sorrow.
I ask you this in the name of Jesus,
whose own death brought life.
Amen.

Prayer for a Dying Spouse

God who never abandons us,
my beloved is dying.
How can we say good-bye?
With family and friends around us,
we once vowed to love
"as long as we both shall live."
Now I want to stretch that vow,
to once again pledge to love "forever."
Death has no power to extinguish love.
I will continue to give my partner my heart,
even though it is broken.
Loving God, author of life,
please give me the courage and the words
to say good-bye.
Thy will be done.
Amen.

On Starting Over after the Loss of a Spouse

God of new beginnings,
each day dawns differently now.
My beloved has died,
and yet lives in a legacy of grace,
in meaning and memory,
in wisdom that was shared.
These forever gifts remind me
that I am not yet single.
I have been a married person,
and I am still in love.
As my life goes on, God,
help me become aware
of the new places you choose for me
in which to share my life.
My future is in your hands.
Amen.

Death of a Child

Lord,
we are devastated by the death of ________________.
We find it is difficult
to deal with tragedies of this magnitude.
It feels as if this is not real
and we do not know what to say or do.
Lord, we pray for ________________.
May she/he be at complete peace and joy with you in heaven.
We pray for the family.
Although there is no making sense of this death,
we pray that the Holy Spirit will be with them,
empowering them with all that they need
during this most difficult time.
May they also find comfort through the gestures of love
offered to them from a loving community.
Amen.

Miscarriage

God of comfort,
You who are mother and father of us all,
hear my anguish at the loss of my child.
My heart and body are broken,
wracked with pain and grief.
Let me bring you my cries and my confusion,
my anger and my envy,
my guilt and my sorrow,
knowing that you mourn with me,
that my tears are not wept alone.

You who call us each by name
from our mother's womb
know the wonder of life,
no matter how small,
no matter how young.
Help me to trust
that you will hold my baby in your hands
as I hold this child in my heart.

Your love is wide enough for my pain.
Your healing is the hope I cling to.
Be with me in my pain,
in this present darkness.
Enfold me in your embrace,
and heal my deepest loss.
Amen.

Miscarriage

Merciful God,
the loss of my baby weighs heavily on me.
I am overcome with grief and pain.
Unlike other experiences of death,
I have no photos or other memorabilia
to provide comfort.
Hold me to the hope
that my baby rests now with you,
and that, in time, some form of life
will arise in my family and in me.
With trust in your loving care, I pray.
Amen.

A Prayer for a Grieving Family

O Lord,
come and be present with this family.
Comfort them in their loss,
hold them in their sorrow
and sustain them through their grief.
Enfold them all with your love, Lord
that they may rest within your arms.
Watch over their sleep
and take their hands each morning
as they face a new day.
Bind their hearts as one
and bless their relationships.
Might they be united in their loss
but also blessed with smiles and goodness.
Lead this precious family onwards
to embrace life together,
yet hold onto the promise of heaven.
Amen.

Keep me safe,
my God,
for in you I take refuge.
Psalm 16.1

Different Types of Death

Praying with Someone Grieving Loss from Suicide

O God,
from whom nothing can ever separate us,
my dearest *(name of suicide survivor)* is in your hands.
Surround him/her with the light of your love
and with assurances of love and safety.
Help him/her to find a way to live again
and to know that,
even in the most desperate of situations
and most disastrous of events,
you are there - unseen and unheard, perhaps,
but nevertheless present and active
in our broken and hurting lives.
These requests I make
in the name of the One
who came that we might live anew.
Amen.

Suicide

Oh Lord! I should have seen it coming. My loved one [N.] has been living on the edge for years. Help me to forgive my own blindness. Help me to forgive my failure to see suicide was a possibility. Help me to know that [N.] probably wanted us to be blind so s/he could end their life without anyone preventing that end. Help me to know that I probably couldn't have prevented it even if I had known.

[N.] suffered in ways beyond our understanding. S/he did not see the many ways their death would impact us. Suicide left holes in the lives of many. We will carry that pain into the future.

Heal our wounds, dear Lord. Help us to remember the good times that we shared with [N.]. Welcome [N.] into your heavenly kingdom to finally find your love and peace in ways they could not discover in this broken world. Give [N.] the fullness of eternal life and bring healing to those s/he left behind. Amen.

Prayer for One Who Died Accidentally or Violently

Father of mercy,
your compassion is abundant
and reaches to the ends of the earth;
in your kindness
receive our brother/sister ______________
who was suddenly taken from us.
Wash away his/her sins
and bind up his/her wounds;
Welcome him/her at the banquet of love.
Console our heartache,
calm our confusion,
and strengthen our trust
in your great mercy.
Amen.

Prayer at a Time of National or Local Tragedy

Spirit of Love,
be with us as we struggle to make sense
of this terrible tragedy.
Let us know your reassuring presence,
and show us how to provide
consolation and care
for one another
during these fearful and trying days.
Bless all of those who have suffered loss and trauma.
May your healing grace restore balance
and provide hope in the midst of heartache.
Above all, make us mindful of your power
to replace hatefulness with compassion,
violence with peace,
and discord with harmony.
Amen.

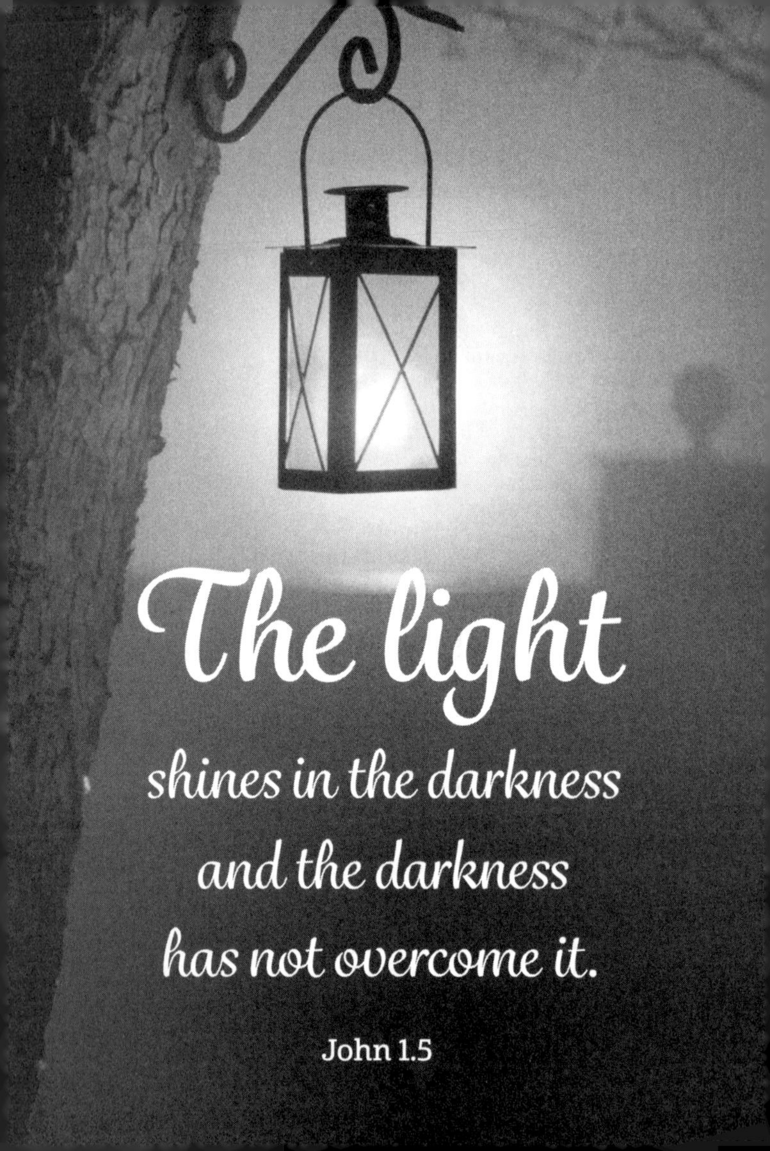
The light
shines in the darkness
and the darkness
has not overcome it.
John 1.5

Special Days of Commemoration

All Saints (November 1)

In Gratitude for the Saints

Dear God,
today we give you thanks for all our saints.
They have provided us
with a wonderful living witness to your love.
They have faithfully followed you
and in so doing touched the lives
of so many here on earth.
Lord, help us to follow the example of our saints.
May we be granted the faith and discipline
to follow in their footsteps.
Amen.

We Pray with the Saints

God of all time and all space,
we thank you and we praise you.
Together with all the saints,
all good and holy people,
we are joined together
by your goodness, truth and wisdom.
We also give thanks
for all those holy men and women
who shine with their living examples
of your faith, hope and love.
This we pray in Jesus' name.
Amen.

Our Home Is among the Saints

Holy God,
through the arms of your saints,
you embrace the whole world
in your love.
May we always know
that we belong to you,
that our true home is among the saints,
and that we are a blessed people
among other blessed people.
We make this prayer
in the name of Jesus.
Amen.

Communion of Saints

O God,
the community of the saints offers us
a model of holiness and helpers on the journey.
Thank you for their witness,
whether on a grand scale
or in small and simple ways.
May we turn to them in times of need
and follow their example when the journey is difficult.
When our earthly days are ended,
we look forward in hope to sharing with them
the light of eternal life.
All you holy women and men, pray for us!
Amen.

All Souls' Day (November 2)

Dear God,
today we remember
our relatives and friends who have died.
We miss them dearly
and wish that they were here with us.
Help us to get through our sorrow.
Our grieving is a sign of our love for them.
We know that we were blessed
with these people in our lives,
and that they continue to live on in us.
God, may we be comforted today
in knowing that our loved ones are at peace,
in your embrace,
and that one day we will see them again.
Amen.

Jesus, by your Resurrection
you have conquered death.
May the souls of those whose passing
we have mourned,
especially our family members and colleagues,
rejoice in the glory of life everlasting.
May our own lives,
whether they be long or short,
be shining examples of compassion and hope.
Lead us forward together in the light of your truth.
Amen.

God our Father,
your power brings us to birth,
your providence guides our lives,
and by your command we return to dust.
Lord, those who die still live in your presence;
their lives change but do not end.
I pray in hope for my family, relatives and friends,
and for all the dead known to you alone.
In company with Christ,
who died and now lives,
may they rejoice in your kingdom,
where all our tears are wiped away.
Unite us together again in one family,
to sing your praise forever and ever.
Amen.

Prayers for Remembrance Day (Canada) or Veterans Day (USA)

Prayers for November 11

O God,
our help and our shield,
thank you for the courageous service
of all those who have died as a result of war.
Comfort those who have suffered their loss.
Watch over all who are serving in uniform today.
Show all of us how to work together
to build a world where war is no more,
and forgive us when we fall short.
Guide the leaders of nations
to make decisions based on justice and compassion
rather than greed or lust for power.
Help us learn to be peacemakers
in our words and our actions.
Amen.

Dear Lord,
we remember today all those
who fought for peace and justice.
No words can fully express
the appreciation we have for all those
who have made sacrifices
and continue to make sacrifices.
Bless them, Lord!
Many gave their lives
to thwart the cruelty and evil of dictators
and to establish equality, freedom and peace.
For those who have died,
we pray that they be with you in peace and joy,
and that their families find comfort and peace.
Amen.

The Lord is my shepherd, I shall not want.

Psalm 23.1

Psalms

Psalm 23

The Divine Shepherd

The Lord is my shepherd, I shall not want.
He makes me lie down in green pastures;
he leads me beside still waters;
he restores my soul.
He leads me in right paths
for his name's sake.

Even though I walk through the darkest valley,
I fear no evil;
for you are with me;
your rod and your staff –
they comfort me.

You prepare a table before me
in the presence of my enemies;
you anoint my head with oil;
my cup overflows.

Surely goodness and mercy shall follow me
all the days of my life,
and I shall dwell in the house of the Lord
my whole life long.

Psalm 25

Prayer for Guidance and for Deliverance

To you, O Lord, I lift up my soul.
O my God, in you I trust;
do not let me be put to shame;
do not let my enemies exult over me.
Do not let those who wait for you be put to shame;
let them be ashamed who are wantonly treacherous.

Make me to know your ways, O Lord;
teach me your paths.
Lead me in your truth, and teach me,
for you are the God of my salvation;
for you I wait all day long.

Be mindful of your mercy, O Lord, and of your steadfast love,
for they have been from of old.
Do not remember the sins of my youth or my transgressions;
according to your steadfast love remember me,
for your goodness' sake, O Lord!

Good and upright is the Lord;
therefore he instructs sinners in the way.
He leads the humble in what is right,
and teaches the humble his way.
All the paths of the Lord are steadfast love and faithfulness,
for those who keep his covenant and his decrees.

For your name's sake, O Lord,
pardon my guilt, for it is great.
Who are they that fear the Lord?
He will teach them the way that they should choose.

➝

They will abide in prosperity,
and their children shall possess the land.
The friendship of the Lord is for those who fear him,
and he makes his covenant known to them.
My eyes are ever toward the Lord,
for he will pluck my feet out of the net.

Turn to me and be gracious to me,
for I am lonely and afflicted.
Relieve the troubles of my heart,
and bring me out of my distress.

Consider my affliction and my trouble,
and forgive all my sins.
Consider how many are my foes,
and with what violent hatred they hate me.
O guard my life, and deliver me;
do not let me be put to shame, for I take refuge in you.
May integrity and uprightness preserve me,
for I wait for you.

Redeem Israel, O God,
out of all its troubles.

The name of the Lord is a strong tower, the righteous run into it and are safe.

Proverbs 18.10

Psalm 31

Prayer and Praise for Deliverance from Enemies

In you, O Lord, I seek refuge;
do not let me ever be put to shame;
in your righteousness deliver me.
Incline your ear to me;
rescue me speedily.
Be a rock of refuge for me,
a strong fortress to save me.

You are indeed my rock and my fortress;
for your name's sake lead me and guide me,
take me out of the net that is hidden for me,
for you are my refuge.
Into your hand I commit my spirit;
you have redeemed me, O Lord, faithful God.

You hate those who pay regard to worthless idols,
but I trust in the Lord.
I will exult and rejoice in your steadfast love,
because you have seen my affliction;
you have taken heed of my adversities,
and have not delivered me into the hand of the enemy;
you have set my feet in a broad place.

Be gracious to me, O Lord, for I am in distress;
my eye wastes away from grief,
my soul and body also.
For my life is spent with sorrow,
and my years with sighing;
my strength fails because of my misery,
and my bones waste away.

→

I am the scorn of all my adversaries,
a horror to my neighbors,
an object of dread to my acquaintances;
those who see me in the street flee from me.
I have passed out of mind like one who is dead;
I have become like a broken vessel.
For I hear the whispering of many –
terror all around! –
as they scheme together against me,
as they plot to take my life.

But I trust in you, O Lord;
I say, "You are my God."
My times are in your hand;
deliver me from the hand of my enemies and persecutors.
Let your face shine upon your servant;
save me in your steadfast love.

Do not let me be put to shame, O Lord,
for I call on you;
let the wicked be put to shame;
let them go dumbfounded to Sheol.
Let the lying lips be stilled
that speak insolently against the righteous
with pride and contempt.

➞

O how abundant is your goodness
that you have laid up for those who fear you,
and accomplished for those who take refuge in you,
in the sight of everyone!
In the shelter of your presence you hide them
from human plots;
you hold them safe under your shelter
from contentious tongues.

Blessed be the Lord,
for he has wondrously shown his steadfast love to me
when I was beset as a city under siege.
I had said in my alarm,
"I am driven far from your sight."
But you heard my supplications
when I cried out to you for help.

Love the Lord, all you his saints.
The Lord preserves the faithful,
but abundantly repays the one who acts haughtily.
Be strong, and let your heart take courage,
all you who wait for the Lord.

Psalm 40

Thanksgiving for Deliverance and Prayer for Help

I waited patiently for the Lord;
he inclined to me and heard my cry.
He drew me up from the desolate pit,
out of the miry bog,
and set my feet upon a rock,
making my steps secure.
He put a new song in my mouth,
a song of praise to our God.
Many will see and fear,
and put their trust in the Lord.

Happy are those who make
the Lord their trust,
who do not turn to the proud,
to those who go astray after false gods.
You have multiplied, O Lord my God,
your wondrous deeds and your thoughts toward us;
none can compare with you.
Were I to proclaim and tell of them,
they would be more than can be counted.

Sacrifice and offering you do not desire,
but you have given me an open ear.
Burnt offering and sin offering
you have not required.
Then I said, "Here I am;
in the scroll of the book it is written of me.
I delight to do your will, O my God;
your law is within my heart."

I have told the glad news of deliverance
in the great congregation;
see, I have not restrained my lips,

➛

as you know, O Lord.
I have not hidden your saving help within my heart,
I have spoken of your faithfulness and your salvation;
I have not concealed your steadfast love and your faithfulness
from the great congregation.

Do not, O Lord, withhold
your mercy from me;
let your steadfast love and your faithfulness
keep me safe forever.
For evils have encompassed me
without number;
my iniquities have overtaken me,
until I cannot see;
they are more than the hairs of my head,
and my heart fails me.

Be pleased, O Lord, to deliver me;
O Lord, make haste to help me.
Let all those be put to shame and confusion
who seek to snatch away my life;
let those be turned back and brought to dishonor
who desire my hurt.
Let those be appalled because of their shame
who say to me, "Aha, Aha!"

But may all who seek you
rejoice and be glad in you;
may those who love your salvation
say continually, "Great is the Lord!"

As for me, I am poor and needy,
but the Lord takes thought for me.
You are my help and my deliverer;
do not delay, O my God.

Biblical Verses

Blessed are those who mourn,
for they shall be comforted.
(Matthew 5.4)

We shall always be with the Lord.
(1 Thessalonians 4.17)

Jesus, remember me
when you come into your kingdom.
(Luke 23.42)

Lord Jesus, receive my spirit.
(Acts 7.59)

Let not your hearts be troubled.
Believe in God; believe also in me.
In my Father's house are many rooms.
If it were not so,
would I have told you
that I go to prepare a place for you?
And if I go and prepare a place for you,
I will come again and will take you to myself,
that where I am you may be also.
And you know the way to where I am going.
(John 14.1-4)

Whether we live or die,
we are the Lord's.
(Romans 14.8)

The Lord is near to the broken hearted
and saves the crushed in spirit.
(Psalm 34.18)

Trust in the Lord with all your heart,
and do not lean on your own understanding.
(Proverbs 3.5)

For I am sure that neither death nor life,
nor angels nor rulers,
nor things present nor things to come,
nor powers, nor height nor depth,
nor anything else in all creation,
will be able to separate us
from the love of God
in Christ Jesus our Lord.
(Romans 8.38-39)

Special Memories

My Special Prayer

Sources

pp. 9, 11, 27, 29, 34, 39 – Timothy Johnston, *Pocket Prayers for Times of Trouble.* New London: Twenty-Third Publications, 2014.

pp. 11, 25, 26, 28, 33, 41, 43, 44, 45 – Filomena Tassi and Peter Tassi, *365 Prayers for Catholic Schools and Parish Youth Groups.* Toronto: Novalis, 2016.

pp. 17, 18, 19, 20 – Janet Schaeffler, SND, *A Treasury of Marian Prayers: A Handbook of Popular Devotions.* New London: Twenty-Third Publications, 2017.

p. 21 – *Prayers to Mary: Words of Beauty and Wisdom: Living with Christ special issue.* Toronto: Novalis, 2019.

pp. 23, 31, 32, 33 – Patricia Hughes Baumer and Fred A. Baumer, *Pocket Prayers for Married Couples.* New London: Twenty-Third Publications, 2015.

pp. 24, 43, 44, 45 – Krystyna Higgins, *Inviting God: Simple, Creative Prayers for Meetings.* Toronto: Novalis, 2018.

p. 25 – Julie Rattey, *Pocket Prayers for Young Professionals.* New London: Twenty-Third Publications, 2013.

pp. 27, 32, 35, 39 – Kathy Hendricks, *Pocket Prayers for Parents.* Toronto: Novalis, 2014.

p. 38 – Glen Argan. Used with permission.

p. 42 – Lisa Freemantle and Les Miller, *Words for the Journey for Kids: Ten-Minute Prayer Services for Schools.* Toronto: Novalis, 2010.